Another book by Pius Yao Ashiara

The Corridor of Life

The GREATMIND Marriage Theater

THE GOSPEL OF MARRIAGE

PIUS Y. ASHIARA

ARCHWAY
PUBLISHING

Archway Publishing books may be ordered through booksellers or by contacting:

Archway Publishing
1663 Liberty Drive
Bloomington, IN 47403
www.archwaypublishing.com
1 (888) 242-5904

ISBN: 978-1-4808-3270-1 (sc)
ISBN: 978-1-4808-3272-5 (hc)
ISBN: 978-1-4808-3271-8 (e)

Library of Congress Control Number: 2016909718

Print information available on the last page.

Archway Publishing rev. date: 7/13/2016

CONTENTS

GOOD CHOICE

For a good marriage to work,

Choice! Choice! Choice!

Is it beauty? No!

Is it wealth? No!

Is it solidarity? Yes!

Is it kindness and respect? Yes!

Is it happiness? Yes! Yes! Yes,

but choice, choice, choice

is best to consider.

But first look at the heart.

– Pius Yao Ashiara

WITH LOVE AND GRATITUDE:

Mr. Kwasi Hughes

Mrs. Esi Hughes

PREFACE

Marriage is a very tall mountain we climb,

but not everyone can climb it to the top.

— Pius Yao Ashiara

God gave us the mountain to take our marriages to the greatest heights, but only a few make that climb. Many settle for the hill and never enjoy the scenery of the earth that is best obtained from the top of a mountain.

Many married men or women let disappointment, regret, pain, hate and bitterness become a chain in the marriage to bind them to one place and never reach Mount Everest.

One Way Street sign

Marriage is only one way, and everyone has only one trip in life. Therefore every marriage must be only one trip too. Marriage is like the two hands. The signs in the palms are different from every other person's. These signs are our fate; if we will study and understand what they mean and follow their meaning we will make fewer mistakes in life. Marriage is not for today, but for the *future*. The early years of marriage are a bloomed flower. Unless you keep attention on it and water it constantly as it grows, it will wilt in no time. Look about you and see what is happening to many marriages, and you wonder how people understand the "marriage vow" before going into marriage.

In the media, and television and the courts, the wrong in marriage is being brought to the public eye, which makes marriage a scary business to some. Many married couples, or a man or a woman, no longer respect marriage and have turned marriage into a "sex ball game." Many are looking for only a few minutes of pleasure as opposed to a lifetime of happiness in marriage. Many are taking a few minutes of pleasure to destroy their own marriage and a few minutes to destroy another person's marriage and happiness.

It is more appropriate for people to stay single and pursue their sex pleasures than to pretend being married and then abuse the marriage, which blasphemes God.

Marriage is an investment, but friendship is the floor to study each other before signing on to it. Marriage is jealous and forbids repetition, but it encourages continuity. No new performer. The only thing people can see outside of it should be its children holding a flag thanking their parents or guardians in their adulthood. The flowers we take to a wedding tell us that marriage is a beautiful thing and has to be decorated and kept clean throughout its life.

Good choice makes a successful marriage: When you go into a store to shop for clothes, the first thing you consider before purchasing is the quality of the material and its longevity. And next is the price of what you are buying. That is why we shop around before we purchase goods and services. More so, that is what we must do before marrying another person – we must consider choice or we may end up buying a lemon. A good choice that matches one's taste saves the future of marriage.

Make a thorough search when picking a mate. Marriage is like buying a car from a dealership. The car you select will determine how far you can go in your journey in your life.

Making a good choice is like putting bitumen on a rough road. It makes traveling easier in the future. Unfortunately, some choices we make in selecting a mate are like trying to affix wood to a metal. Such selections make marriage mechanical and never work. Seventy-five percent of our lives is invested in marriage; that is why a good selection is important to go with it.

This work is prepared for a man and woman as a mirror in which they must see themselves before getting into marriage.

INTRODUCTION

People in the western world are great workers. They work with a tremendous energy and perseverance. They put great thinking and concentration into their lives. They hold their time to the clock with great care so that nothing distracts them from their goals. Anyone who would put thinking and time into his life will be a progressive person in the world. Secondly, it will enable him have an organized economy and his finances will be the best (*finances* and *marriage* determine a person's success or failure in life).

The Western world holds four priorities in life they never take for granted: thinking, time, finances and child care. These make them progressive people of the world.

Many people take marriage as new cooking pot bought from the store to cook. It is new in the store, so we find it attractive and buy it instantly. We reach home before we realize that there is nothing in it to our benefit. This is the same way we choose a woman or a man for marriage. It is only then we try to fill the person with training before we can obtain anything good for our use.

Before we marry anyone, we must consider our choice as a uniform in the store that we want to buy. Before we buy it, we must turn it "inside" out and take a thorough look at it and take a good look at the "face" (front) before we decide on our choice.

In life, it is important to lay a foundation with the essential things from the beginning and end of our lives. Before we court friendship with a man or a woman, it is important that we put it into writing, so that things that come up later in the relationship will be binding on both parties (in case pregnancy occurs or a child is born without the backing of a legal document). Everyone born must have a legal backing by law. There should be some form of legal document binding the relationship so that a child is not born without the involvement of a father. Naturally, a father is not obliged to use a stroller, but he is endowed with ability to train a child; that is why it requires his presence as a father at training. A mother has only two hands, but with a father's two hands, they have four hands on all corners of a child. Childcare and domestic chores when they overwhelm a mother, they turn her into a nag and complainer. Unless she gets help there will never be peace in the home.

Thirdly, a woman in the relationship should know the future career of the man in the relationship. This awareness should come before the relationship begins. The world is full of irresponsible lives, and this approach protects a woman from facing the job alone in the future.

CHAPTER 1

Man

If you are a man, you are going to be two persons in the future (a man and a husband). That is why you must lay a foundation for yourself. Stop! Think! And ask yourself some important questions before you continue your life's journey. If you are man you have a significant work ahead of you that you must pursue with earnestness. Now you must take your life with a career or profession and move on. Let your hands and feet move quickly. Your plan should be organized to be moving forward always through the years of your life and be on the lookout always for your growth. Train yourself to be an able man or a warrior who is always prepared for emergencies. This will get you ready if the need should arise. Make room always for your happiness, and this will put energy and enthusiasm into your life. If you are a man, you must train yourself an indefatigable worker with perseverance. You cannot be a lazy man, because in the future you are going to head a household. You ought to train yourself to work with bloodshot eyes.

CHAPTER 2

Husband

The greatest gift a husband can get

is a wife with a good heart and so

a woman with a husband with a

good heart.

— *Pius Yao Ashiara*

Husband: When you become a husband you become three persons (a man, a husband and a wife). When you become a husband, you have a huge responsibility you must accept with open arms. If a child is born into the relationship, you become four persons (a man, a husband, a wife and a child or children). You are no longer one person. And now you have some other person's children under your care. Now you must take your two hands to make your plans for the family. Some men live by only "one hand." Such men are lazy. Some men chase money and property with the right hand while driving the wife and children away with the left hand. This is not acceptable in marriage. It means they put material possession ahead of the marriage. *You cannot put anything before or above your marriage.* Some husbands keep their wives behind or cover them with "basket" like a cat, so that they have no say or voice in their marriage. This is wrong from husbands, since all of them are married couples and they ought to be on the same page all the time. You must have a safe and comfortable and a joyful home (Fig. 2.1). Your bed and where you and your wife sleep, and that of your children, should be the most superb place in your home for relaxation and resting. There must be a place for a good sound system with good music playing all the times. So must be a library with every kind of book for your daily reading and use of your family.

A picture of a comfortable bed.

When you are a husband with a son, know that your son is going to be married to someone's daughter. You have to train this son with the duties of a man and a husband and homework to grow with it into adulthood. Most important is to train him with responsibilities with great care as head of household. If he has younger siblings, bring him to learn how to train them as well with homework and family duties into adulthood. This would promote solidarity and love of mankind in his life. Teach them the worship of God from childhood to grow with it into adulthood. Teach them respect (humility) for all people and the good care of money and how to use money from childhood. Guide them in childhood to discover a profession or a career or a goal to be a vision in front of them to hold in hand into adulthood. It should be the same training for his sisters if he has any.

When you are a husband, show your wife and other people that you are her backbone, a great force behind her. So must a wife do for a husband.

A thing to note: *After children have grown to be on their own is when the true character of a father becomes apparent.*

CHAPTER 3

Failure of a Husband in Marriage

The Failure of a Husband in Marriage: A married man's success comes from a wife, whether in business or life. A hard working husband can fail if he is not wholly supported by a wife, especially if the wife only thinks of material things without the care of savings. The whole world wonders about such a hard working man who has worked all his life without the involvement of the wife in his goal, especially when both partners started their marriage from the very bottom of life. It is important that a husband determines the course of their direction and where it is leading them financially. At times a wife can take control of the marriage and drive it into a financial ruin. A husband must turn himself into a "golfer" in the marriage so that his eyes and mind are on their money and expenditures; otherwise he will make a poor score as a man. The tendency to spend is more flexible in many wives' hands than husbands, especially when the wife is making less money or not working at all.

What a married man should not do. He should not go with another woman or another man's wife; he must not have an affair outside the marriage that brings another child into the marriage; he must not make drink (Fig. 2.2) **his companion and must always tell the wife the truth in all matters and must be depended upon and must respect the wife wherever they are. So must be the wife.**

Every life is only once; therefore every marriage must be only once, especially when the marriage has produced children. If a spouse spoils the marriage, he or she has ruined a life. It is not advisable to repeat marriage especially when children are involved.

The success of a husband in marriage: Doing what the wife likes and always seeking her interest. He must be available at all times for her and his children. Making sure the needs of his home are met. He is proud of his wife and compliments her on her dressing and cooking. He is a father, but not just a man. He treats the wife as a queen and respects her inside the home and more especially when they are outside the home. Apart from God, she comes next. He must take God as a partner in the marriage and seeking the best out of her. He must become a "supervisor," making sure that all her needs are met and her car is in good running condition and offering his services wherever it is needed and always bringing her flowers (not only when he has done wrong and apologizes). A wife must do the same thing for the husband.

CHAPTER 4

Woman

FICTION

Woman: If you are a woman, you are going to be three persons in the future (a woman, a wife and a husband); that is why you must lay a solid foundation for yourself and be ready for the onslaught. Stop! Think!

Before you continue your journey of life, ask yourself one question. If you are a woman, you have a very important role to play. The care of the HOME faces you. You must make plans for childcare. Know that a wife is different from a husband and train for childcare.

Before you marry, check the background of the parents of the person you want to marry (husband and wife). They will be the mirror to look into to see what will be coming to you in your own marriage (Fig. 4.1).

The kind of life the parents of your partner have led will reflect upon their son or daughter – this helps a great deal in your marriage decision.

A Picture of Mirror

CHAPTER 5

Wife

When you become a wife, you will become two persons in the future (a wife and a husband); if a child is born into the marriage, you will be three persons (a wife, a husband and a child). You must learn to cook very well to be the provider of the HOME. You must learn to cook with joy and enthusiasm, making yourself in charge of the kitchen. A kitchen is like sanctuary for a wife. You must do this with pride and happiness. You must be prepared to embrace your husband's career or profession and support him in every way within your power. Your husband's career or work is going to meet the expenses of the home, you and the children, if any. Learn personality grooming, which will be the "flower" and "ornament" to your personality. This will attract your husband to you always.

Before deciding to marry, we must take account of ourselves to see how well prepared we are to marry. Marriage is selling "oneself" to a woman or a man. The question to ask oneself is: What good things are within me to sell to another person? If it happens I should marry someone, what good things do I have to add to make a good marriage? If I don't have anything, I have one important question to answer for myself, that is: Marriage has an end or every life has death (Fig. 5.1).

Dead End

An important thing to answer is: We must have some training or education that will give us income for everyday meals and its financial needs. We must have work before we marry. Marriage is like the marketplace or going to the marketplace to shop. We ought to be holding money in our hands for an exchange of goods and services before we can buy anything. So is marriage.

We must be holding something in our hands that will establish the marriage.

In marriage, some partners are like already-made oversized clothes that are bought in the store and have to be altered before they fit to our size. Some are also undersized, but we must buy them and make adjustments to fit us. In some marriages, if a man doesn't move or take action, a wife does not take action either.

The work of a wife — a wife's work must not take too much of her time or take her from domestic duties. The work of a wife should be a light job to aid that of the husband. Because of childcare and care of the home, a wife's work doesn't require too many hours or a leadership role. It is in old age before we see the training or education we put into our children. There is a reward parents and guardians receive at sickness or retirement if they train or educate their children, who become responsible adults.

Your Children: When you are a wife with a daughter, know that your daughter is going to be married to someone's son. You have to train this daughter with duties of a wife and a mother and homework to grow with it into adulthood. Most important is to teach her the responsibilities of homemaking, with great care as a mother of a home. If she has young siblings, bring her to learn how to train them as well with homework and family duties into adulthood. This will make her grow with solidarity and love of mankind in her life. Teach her respect for all people and the good care of money and how to use money from childhood. It should be the same training for her brothers, if she has any.

When you are a wife, show your husband and other people that you are his backbone: a great force behind him. So must a husband do for a wife.

A thing to note: *After children have grown to be on their own is when the true character of a wife becomes apparent.*

CHAPTER 6

The Failure of a Wife in Marriage

The failure of a wife in marriage: An ambitious wife can fail if she is not supported wholly by her husband to train for some career for the future of their marriage. A forward-looking wife cares about the expenditure of the home. She should be strong on "savings" so that they are always prepared for emergencies, in case something happens to a husband or any of the children. Some wives wish visitors to their homes would go away with only good impressions of their home to talk about – that is why they are strict with the care of their home. A good care and proper decoration of the home are major concerns of some wives; that is why they require the support of a husband in maintenance of the home. Some wives care more about new clothes every time there is an outing and make sure that their desire is met.

In many instances such wives do not have any education or training or income to be able to take over the expenses of the family, in case something happens to husband.

A wife needs to be Bank Savings savvy. A wife and a husband need to make a strong provision for the home and financial savings as the foundation for the marriage. Some wives prefer buying everything on credit thus they don't have any cash for savings. A loving wife is vigilant about what comes out of the husband's pocket. Another thing a wife ought to do is respect her husband. She must recognize that he is the head of the household and its success belongs to him. This will make their children respect their father as well. There is a serious lack of respect for many husbands coming from wives these days in marriages. A man's place is the head, and no one can take away his respect. It is something God established for man at the dawn of history. Oh, woman! Your hands are made two; that is why you need to raise your children with a man. No woman can say she doesn't need a man in her life. God made two hands for the two partners because two persons (a man and a woman) make a child.

What a married woman should not do in marriage. She should not go with another man or a woman's husband; she should not be envious of another woman's husband; she must not make drink her companion. She must always tell her husband the truth in all matters and must respect him and show it wherever they are.

Every life is only once; therefore every marriage must be only once, especially when the marriage has produced children. If a spouse spoils the marriage, he or she has ruined a life. It is not advisable to repeat marriage, especially when children are involved.

The success of a wife in marriage: There is nothing a husband cherishes more than respect coming from his wife and his children. A man in general likes an obedient and humble woman, whether she is single or married.

She likes a well-dressed husband who is neat and likes to hold him high before others as the president. A good thing a wife can do to win the husband's heart is make sure he receives the best meals and she is at his service always. A humble wife wins a husband to her own taste. When you are woman and you come on "too strong," men will date you, but they will not marry you. You may have a boyfriend for a relationship, but he will keep you for only a "taste" and not for a wife. He will do this as a man to kill your ego as a woman with laughter.

A wife is a mirror for the husband. Before he leaves home, she inspects her husband's dressing to make sure his appearance is appealing to the eye, and so should a husband do for the wife.

Before we marry, we must know and understand married love:

What is love? Love is like a baby we raise to growth (Fig. 6.1).

Baby

True love grows slowly. Happiness and patience are the water that makes it grow. We have to lay a foundation for it to grow with things that make it last – seeking the best out of the other person with love, respect, helpfulness, gratitude, kindness, compliments and praise, and grooming always. Love is like a flame that does not die (Fig. 6.2).

A Burning Flame

We need to put the right things into it to make it smolder all the time. Love is breakable. It is more precious than gold and silver. When we take it, we must develop it to grow wider and deeper than the ocean. It is like a seed that is nurtured and tended before it grows into a fruit (Fig. 6.3).

Orange and Orange seeds

Love is like a house that must start with a concrete foundation or a tree with roots to hold it in one place. Love is music in our hearts; unless one sings it, no one enjoys it. It sparkles like a diamond. Nothing will tarnish it if it is genuine.

In marriage, a husband must guide his wife to be independent so that if sickness or death comes to the husband, she will not be left wanting.

Life is a journey trodden by many, and where those coming after can find the proper path to walk through.

Some women develop an "outside" relationship where pregnancy comes from another man, which is a great wrong a woman does in marriage. So does a man also has a child "outside" a marriage, which is a wrong done by a man too. Animals live like that, so if you live this way don't consider yourself a human being. We should be careful to prevent such wrongs from our marriage. Marriage is a thing of the heart. When it is hurt, it creates an open wound on the heart. No surgeon can operate its wound. And no surgery can heal its wound. It is a thing of the heart and its foundation cannot be laid on falsehood. If it is built on falsehood, it is standing on sand, but if it is built on a genuine love, its foundation is built with a concrete that cannot break into pieces. Pain in the heart is a thorn. But many do not consider the wrong they do to inflict a wound on another's heart. Every married heart seeks happiness and joy. You cannot put pain on another's heart and think you are a free person. You imprison your own heart in a cage that is locked forever.

There is curse that comes from God in punishing a wrongdoer on account of the vow both parties have sworn to in the marriage.

Hey, wife! Do you observe the wedding gown you wore today? This is the prescription for your marriage forever, to keep clean all the time until your death. Hey, husband! Do you observe the tuxedo you have worn today? This is the prescription for your marriage forever, to keep clean all the time until your death. Some women regard their marriage as their "heaven," which they don't take for granted, and stay by it day and night.

Life is a short journey that requires us to take with it "good things" that makes life pleasant and successful. It requires us to pause from time to time to reflect upon our performance in our marriage and life. As we go, we must set a measurement for our performance and correct where we go wrong. In marriage, we should not turn our ears to listen to others to take charge of our relationship. We have to make our own plans to follow. What an individual plans usually works better.

Almighty Everlasting God built the Garden of Eden for man and woman to be their salvation, happiness, gladness, joy, and a place to care for children. The sins of mankind make us ignore what a grand life God has given us. The Garden of Eden is Heaven created for us to live by, that is the earth on which we live. In it we must serve Him also with a good life.

What is marriage? It is the vow a husband and wife (man and woman) took to be together in love until death. Marriage starts with a woman's white wedding gown with a ring and a man's wedding tuxedo with a ring.

Decoration, flowers, (Fig. 6.4) prayers, singing, dancing, applause, laughter, different kinds of exotic dishes,

A Flower Bouquet

assorted drinks, cake, and compliments from onlookers accompany this special occasion. Mothers, fathers, siblings, relatives, friends, the clergy, and fellow workers come from far and near distances to celebrate this important day. Joy and excitement accompany the celebration. Yes! This is the way the marriage should stay until its end. The married couple makes a vow with the (Fig. 6.5) **BIBLE** to each other in the presence of a clergy. Photographers take pictures to commemorate the event. These photographs become a souvenir for the family.

A Picture of the BIBLE

Moving forward is progress. It is then wrong to turn and look back and say, "Had I known, I should not have married this person." Marriage is eternal bliss. Love, happiness, togetherness, and childcare with all our energy is its task. An investment or the greatest work that is never taken for granted in life is marriage -- that is why we must study each other before the consummation of a marriage.

The three essential things we should investigate about the person we want to marry:

1. **How does he/she think or reason?** – Thinking and reasoning make us humans and make us pay attention to our life, which helps us make less mistakes in life;

2. **How does he/she invest in time?** – Human beings have a short time to live and with that we do all things;

3. **How does he/she handle money?** – Money makes us leave home every day for our jobs. Good care allows us meet our needs.

These three things are the "building blocks" of marriage.

In the world at large, from North to South, from East to West, from Africa to America, from South America to India, from Great Britain to China, from Germany to Russia, marriage is the same for all people, and its flag is raised high with joy and happiness everywhere and every day. But one law holds all — that is the voice of God that follows the vow of the marriage. We are warned not to let material things, riches, and avarice supersede the marriage.

We live only once; that is why it is ideal to marry only once, which will make our journey through life pleasant. If the marriage fails, it is good to revive it, but it is not wise to go into marriage twice or several times. There is Heaven and Hell; that is why it is essential that we handle it well. Holding each other's hands always strengthen it and must be carried out through the life of the marriage.

If you are a woman, study the qualities of men well, and so must a man study the qualities of women well. Of woman, a man must know her jealousies, envy, glooming, and what children mean to her. Some women are not trained to take charge of their own life and neither also are some men. If we marry these type of persons, thinking to change them in the future, we will be disappointed. You cannot bend an old tree, and so you cannot change an elderly person.

One important thing to note about a marriage partner is "conscience" or a "debilitating character." A person with good conscience would hardly hurt others and thinks thoroughly before an act. Before marriage, we must take note of the essential things before we enter into the relationship. We must make sure that the person we are going to marry will keep the marriage through life. It is good to make known to your partner what makes you angry, so that he or she will keep this in mind. Do not wait until after the wedding to reveal such a flaw to your partner. There are various kinds of qualities or character we possess as human beings. It is therefore necessary to sit and discuss such qualities and character before we sign a document on our partnership. This will prevent problems from the marriage in the future.

Next, we must invite God as a guide in our marriage. Marriage is God's creation for mankind. Do not seek the instructions or advice of your father or mother or friends to decide your marriage. Use your judgment or make your own choices as you please.

There are enemies of marriage, so do not leave a "gap" between the union. What works best for a marriage is both partners must live under one roof night and day. Some of our friends are "poison" and wish to see the marriage fail. If we are not careful of those types of friends and they get close to us, they will destroy our marriage. We must identify such problems and avoid them. Some friends, when their marriage fails, wish others to fail as well. Marriage is a breakable union like a plate (Fig. 6.6); that is why it is essential we hold it firmly with our "two hands."

Plate

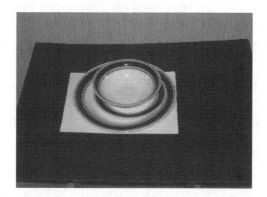

Marriage can bring on humiliation, heartache, headache, atrocities, or death to some persons when they violate its laws.

Often in marriage, an individual partner can bring on heartache or pain to another. We have to ensure that such incident does not occur in ours.

When a man wants to marry, the first thing he identifies is a woman's character; so a woman does as well. She also identifies a man's character; that is why it is appropriate to study "people" early from childhood, which aids us in our decisions in adulthood. One of the important things for the marriage is a woman must train to be a good cook; so must a man. A wife with children does not have enough "time," and this requires a husband to fill some spots in the marriage. A woman needs help in the home when she has children and works outside the home for an income to supplement that of the husband. Now, the cost of living has gone higher, and both partners must work, so it is important a husband must help in domestic duties. Marriage is like a shirt or uniform (Fig. 6.7);

people see only the "face" but not the "inside." Only the good is known to other persons.

A Shirt

We may argue, we may fight, we may exchange blows, but in the public eye we do not let other persons see it, and it is flowers, laughter, joy and compliments even when there are wrongs with it. That is why we take decorations, flowers, applause, laughter, and compliments to begin a marriage.

Life is money God put into our hands to spend
wisely.

-*Pius Yao Ashiara*

An important thing to note is never to owe any debt to anyone if they don't have any savings backing the marriage. If you don't have money saved, at least don't owe anyone. Money and adultery are the most important things that we must pay attention to — these two things destroy marriage. In money matters, a husband and wife must always sit down on their money matters so that the wrong will not come from one person's financial decisions. A wedding ring is required in marriage; that is why we purchase one. But not every partner values it. We must purchase one, but it is not good to purchase it on "credit" or to owe a debt to it. Marriage should not start with debt; it should start with savings because its future is unknown and it is a protection against difficulties.

Some wear the ring against intrusion of outside forces and as a protection against failure.

One thing we must also identify is: It has an end. Some marriages will last until the passing of the partners; some will be short-lived; some, a partner or partners may pass away before its end; some will bring on a fight among persons; some will fail, but will be corrected; some, a partner would walk out on the marriage; some will create hatred among relatives or other persons; some would implore voodoo or a magic spell to rivet a partner's love permanently; some will end by the psychiatrist; some will end at the hospital; some will end in the Court of Justice.

In some marriages when a wife takes a husband as her only hope in life and the man dies too soon, the wife becomes disillusioned and may require some medical attention. At times God may take a loved one from a wife but will blow His breath into her palms with gratuity or insurance money to pacify her to make a new life. While in marriage, it is important that we handle ours well as we seek happiness more than anything else. At times the two partners must sit and reflect on the life of the marriage and identify the wrongs that need to be corrected. Some partners turn the marriage into "bones" for dogs to chew on. The right thing to do in a marriage is to turn it into a "hot iron" that others cannot approach. Marriage is a proud union that grows like a seed. In the presence of others, we hold it as an egg. We have to keep our eyes on ours and identify the "crevices" that it has sustained and try to seal them so that other things cannot have the chance to enter into it. Every partner must stand by the marriage. Vigilance about it drives wrong things from it. We ought to hold the marriage as the only life asset we have that will not fall from our hands. It must be rated higher before all others or we must make it the "bestseller." In marriage, we stand by each other even when things go wrong. Marriage is a journey that is why it requires a "pause" and "reflection" on its direction (Fig. 6.8).

A Picture of Highway

It is a place we receive lessons, but there is no school for it but a union where we teach and correct each other as we go along.

Marriage is a school or a place we study each other; that is why it is necessary that we know each other before we go into marriage. One important thing to note is to put the marriage on a "table" every December, each year, and take a look at its progress and stability.

Vow

A vow is the foundation to marriage. It is the oath we swear to God in Heaven and on Earth that we will live out our promises until death by being loyal to it. When taken firmly, inviting God's guidance, as promised each other, we turn our marriage into a Granite Home and a blessing for our lives. When we violate its laws, it turns to bring on a curse to our life for which there is punishment from God. Nevertheless, build an altar on your heart and always pray with suppliant heart for its success.

Indeed, it failed! It failed! It failed!

Yes, True! It failed! It failed! It failed!

Oh, our marriage has failed.

Oh, it failed when there is no love in it, it failed.

Oh, it failed when there is no happiness in it, it failed.

Oh, it failed when there is no joy in it, it failed.

Oh, it failed when there is no patience in it, it failed.

Oh, it failed when there is no excitement in it, it failed.

Oh, it failed when there is no togetherness in it, it failed.

Oh, it failed when there is no laughter in it, it failed.

Oh, it failed when there is no guiding one another, it failed.

Oh, it failed when there is no setting right one another, it failed.

Oh, it failed when there is no seeking the best for one another, it failed.

Oh, it failed when there is no enthusiasm in it, it failed.

Yes, indeed! If all of the above are missing, it failed! It failed! It failed!

— Pius Yao Ashiara

CHAPTER 7

What marriage does!

What Marriage does!

Marriage makes a person solid!

The order of marriage is: You never take it and withdraw from it. When you enter into it, it is entered forever. Many persons do not understand the idea of marriage before they enter into it. Some persons take it just for the public to appreciate them as married couple, but this is the big mistake persons make in marriage. Sometimes for marriage to work, we have to take a partner (a man or a woman) and train her or him before we have a good match. One fault of a husband or a wife is they want it "soon enough" or consume it as you get it. Life does not grant things that way. It requires years of hard work, patience and perseverance and so is work required of marriage. The right thing to do is a husband and a wife must have similar thinking and goal. Marriage should grow with love, joy and happiness, togetherness plus childcare. Marriage starts with a "Marriage Certificate," (Fig. 7.1) but there is no school for it. We only take it by studying and teaching one another.

A Picture of Marriage Certificate

CITY OF NEWARK, N. J.
OFFICE OF
M. J. FRATANTUNO, M.D.
REGISTRAR OF VITAL STATISTICS

Nº 7945

This is to Certify that the following is correctly copied from a record of Marriage in my office.

DO NOT ACCEPT THIS CERTIFICATE UNLESS THE RAISED SEAL OF THIS BUREAU IS AFFIXED HEREON.

NAME OF HUSBAND	AGE	BIRTHPLACE
Pius Ashiara	30	Ghana

MAIDEN NAME OF WIFE	AGE	BIRTHPLACE	SURNAME BY PRECEDING MARRIAGE IF ANY
	30	Robersonville, N.C.	None

DATE OF MARRIAGE	PLACE OF MARRIAGE	MARRIAGE PERFORMED BY
March 12, 1977	NEWARK, N. J.	Rev.

In Witness Whereof. I have hereunto set my hand and affixed the seal of Bureau of Vital Statistics, Newark, N. J. this 29th day of Oct. A.D. 19 80.

Registrar of Vital Statistics

But its life is very short because of our life span. If we handle it well, it becomes our bliss and Heaven on earth.

Marriage is a crown, (Fig. 7.2) respect and honor adores it.

A Picture of a Crown

Marriage makes a person solid.

We humans are like a tree (Fig. 7.3); that is why we must have roots to hold us in one place -- marriage is the "taproot."

A Picture of a Tree

We humans are like a house; that is why we must have a solid foundation to hold us down in one place.

We humans are like a river; that is why we must have a riverbed to hold us down.

We humans are like a mountain; that is why we must have a valley to hold us down.

We humans are half a person, but marriage makes us whole.

A husband and wife are a prop to each other.

For a husband, a wife is his prop.

For a wife, a husband is her prop. In happiness, there is
someone to share with. In sorrow, there is someone
to lean on.

Hold your marriage as an impeccable wedding gown.

Hold your marriage as an impeccable tuxedo with care
and respect.

When it is besmirched by "dirt," it is pronounced to the
public.

Oh, why did it come out this way? Many persons will ask!

Oh, my friend, marriage is sacred.

Do not besmirch it with "dirt."

Do not hurt it.

Hold it as a crown.

Do not commit adultery in it.

Do not take it by lying.

Do not take it with regret.

Do not take it with gossip.

Do not take it with heartache.

Do not take it with anger.

Do not take it with back-biting.

Do not take it by crying in it.

Do not take it with laziness.

Do not take it with wickedness.

Do not take it with pain.

Do not take it with selfishness.

Do not let your mother pry into it.

Do not let your father pry into it.

Do not let your relatives pry into it.

Do not let your friends pry into it.

Do not take it to the Court of Justice.

Do not let the clergy be involved in it.

Do not let an attorney be involved in it.

Do not let it come before a judge.

Do not let anybody be involved in it – this is the way to keep it serene and peaceful.

Take it with a plan.

Take it with strength.

Take it by thinking always.

Take it with your two hands.

Take it by worshipping God.

Take it with excitement.

Take it with flowers.

Take it with enthusiasm.

Take it with progress.

Take it with celebrations.

Take it with courage.

Take it with a good heart.

Take it by telling the truth.

Take it with loyalty.

Take it with perseverance.

Take it with persistence.

Take it with love that is deeper and wider than the ocean
(Fig. 7.4).

A Picture of the Ocean

Take it with happiness.

Take it with pride.

Take it with patience.

Take it with humility.

Take it by teaching each other.

Take it by guiding one another.

Take it by seeking the best for each other.

Take it with dancing.

Take it with a smile and laughter.

Take it with service to each other.

Protect it!

Stand by it!

Work on it!

Put "fire" into it!

Deliberate on it!

Do your best with it!

Respect it!

Decorate it by compliments!

Make a song for it!

Handle it well to be a "guide" and "envy" for married couples.

– Pius Yao Ashiara

Oh, let us pause a little and reflect on the things we just heard about our marriage and life. Now listen! "Marriage is a 'plate' that breaks."

Marriage is a "plate" that breaks.

Yes, indeed, it is the truth!

Marriage is a "plate" that falls from the hands.

The things those in it take for granted destroy it. That is why the couple must hold it with their four hands so that it will not fall and break. If we let it fall on to the floor from our hands and it breaks, it will be hard to put together. At times we may try to put it together, but it might not work – because a broken item is not easily fixed. The best is to ensure that there are no "wounds." First we must identify things that break it and prepare for them so that they will not happen in our marriage. Adultery, stealing, lying, alcoholism, pressure on a partner, heartaches, money matters, another person's involvement – these are the first things we must note. The most important is adultery, which brings on disgrace, heartache, or murder. Oftentimes, it brings on anger that may make a partner unreasonable when he or she takes revenge as a payoff. The best is to guard it so that no wrong evades it.

– Pius Yao Ashiara

Oh, let us pause a little and reflect on the things we just heard about our marriage and life. Now listen! "Three persons do not marry."

Listen! Listen! Listen!

Three persons do not marry.

Marriage is for only two persons – a *man* and a *woman*.

Your father can advise you, but cannot marry you.

Your mother can advise you, but cannot marry you.

Your siblings can make a choice for you, but cannot marry you.

Your friends can pinpoint a selection for you, but cannot marry you.

Your clergy can pray for you, but cannot marry you.

Your attorney can defend you, but cannot marry you.

The judge can sign your marriage documents, but cannot marry you.

Marriage is for only two persons.

Marriage is for only two persons.

Go in with the "two hands."

Go in with the "two feet."

Master! Mistress! It is the togetherness of only two persons.

Show them the way! Open the door for them!

Leave them alone to work it out on their own.

Whether it is a right or wrong choice, leave them alone.

With caution, involve your "two hands."

With caution, involve your "four hands."

Make a Peaceful Home; Have children; Build wealth into the marriage and you will enjoy bliss and happiness.

— *Pius Yao Ashiara*

Oh, let us pause a little and reflect on the things we just heard about our marriage and life. Now listen! "Marriage is for only two persons."

Marriage is for only two persons – a *man* and a *woman*, but many eyes observe what goes on in it.

Many ears eavesdrop on its activities.

Many mouths discuss it.

Because of the above, we must investigate our choice before we marry.

What is your partner's goal in life?

What kind of life career or profession has your partner chosen for his or her income?

Which kind of school did he or she attend that will benefit him or her?

How does he or she worship God?

How much does he or she drink?

How does she cook?

How does he help?

How does he or she respect people?

How does he or she care for himself or herself?

How does he or she do household chores?

How does he or she receive people?

How does he or she receive your family members?

How did the father perform in his marriage?

How did the mother perform in her marriage?

How does he or she handle money?

(I will repeat this question again.)

How does he or she handle money?

How does he or she understand things?

How does he or she reason?

How does he or she work?

How much does he chase women?

How much does she go with men?

How does he make friends?

Note all these things before you marry!

— Pius Yao Ashiara

Oh, let us pause a little and reflect on the things we just heard about our marriage and life. Now listen! "Marriage is the greatest institution on earth."

The order of marriage is you can take it but you can't leave it!

Marriage is a corporation where there is no salary.

A husband is the Chief Executive Officer and a wife is the Vice President. These two persons and their children formed the corporation.

The salary that is earned is love, happiness, helpfulness, togetherness, and the good children that are brought out of the marriage.

There is a Marriage Certificate for it, but there are no classes or school for it. We get into it and study and teach each other; that is why it is a difficult solidarity.

Before we become a teacher, we must attend classes or school.

Before we become a medical doctor, we must attend classes or medical school.

Before we become a singer, we learn to sing.

But marriage is not any of these things, rather teaching and guiding each other until death. Love, good planning, good heart, perseverance, honesty, togetherness, and the truth keeps it alive.

It is a corporation many persons wish to work in, but not all persons want to enter it. Fear, selfishness, wickedness, and dragging of the feet and holding back make many persons that way.

— Pius Yao Ashiara

Oh, let us pause a little and reflect on the things we just heard about our marriage and life. Now listen! "Marriage is perseverance."

Marriage is perseverance.

Do not put its wrongs in a "show window" for others to observe.

Do not put it on a "cart" for sale.

Do not turn it into a mirror for others to see what is going on.

Oh, My Mother, hear my case!

Oh, My Father, hear my case!

Oh, My Friend, hear my case!

Oh, Clergy, hear my case!

Oh, Attorney, hear my case!

Oh, Judge, hear my case!

Hear me! Hear me! Hear me! -- destroys marriage.

Do not take it by weeping in it.

Do not take it with sympathy.

Do not take it by hurting.

Do not take it with regret.

Do not take it with pain.

Take it with laughter and joy.

Take it with laughter and patience.

Take it with laughter and pride.

Take it with laughter and support.

Take it with Hope in God.

Take it with courage.

Take it as a clean wedding gown.

Take it with decency as a clean tuxedo.

Take it by telling the Truth.

Take it with compliments.

Take it with Service.

Take it by Dancing.

Worship it as a crown with respect.

Build it into a granite wall to be the envy of married couples.

– Pius Yao Ashiara

Oh, let us pause a little and reflect on the things we just heard about our marriage and life. Now listen! "Marriage as an Infant."

Take your marriage as an infant.

Place it on your "lap" and give it a good bath.

Clean its body well to give it strength.

Let all your hands support it all over.

Oh, it is beautiful to admire, but not all persons can handle it.

But if we handle it with care to succeed, people say, "God Blessed Them."

Oh, it is beautiful – they did very well, they would say.

— Pius Yao Ashiara

Oh, let us pause a little and reflect on the things we just heard about our marriage and life. Now listen! "Marriage is teaching and correcting one another."

Marriage is teaching and correcting one another. Some marriages are like shoes (Fig. 7.5).

A Picture of Small and Big Shoes

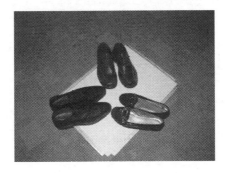

If one is not careful, but the foot gets into the wrong size, it will stop your journey. In the same manner, if your foot gets into a small size, it will leave you at a standstill.

That is why we select a person before we marry. For instance, when you enter a shoe store and see so many shoes of different sizes, you would inquire from the shoe salesperson which shoes will last longer. So is marriage; we must investigate the person who attracts us. Thus it will not turn into an oversize or undersize shoe; similarly we must ensure that the one we pick will not be too tight on our feet and leave us on our door step.

— Pius Yao Ashiara

Oh, let us pause a little and reflect on the things we just heard about our marriage and life. Now listen! "Marrying someone's daughter or son."

Marrying Someone's Daughter or Son

Excuse me, Brothers! Excuse me, Sisters!

Sit and listen to me very well.

If you want to marry a woman or a man and the father or mother says "No! No! No!" three times, you won't marry her; please step back and find another woman or man. **(The word "No" or "Yes" is the strong voice of God in whatever we do. It is important we take them seriously when they occur in our decisions, especially in marriage.)** It is God, who is warning you of future trouble coming to the marriage. This means God didn't sanction the marriage. If you venture and take it, it will be sorrow in your life. What God doesn't sanction we don't fight. The person to marry would say, "Let us ignore my parent or parents and marry." Sometime the person you are fighting to marry changes in the future of the marriage. It is the present opportunity in the marriage that is what she or he is taking advantage of. When you take it with force and a child is born into the relationship, it turns into pain, regret, and sorrow thereafter.

It turns into heartaches!

It turns into headaches!

It turns into anger!

It turns into bitterness!

It turns into, "Oh, if I had known, I would not have married this person."

Or it turns into loss of a life for a partner.

There are lots of women, so are lots of men for choices.

Why fight over a denial by a family?

Brothers and Sisters, take this advice and live with it, so that you would not make a mistake in the future.

—*Pius Yao Ashiara*

Oh, let us pause a little and reflect on the things we just heard about our marriage and life. Now listen! "Love."

Love

Love between two persons is like setting up a campfire together.

Every lover ought to be putting firewood into the flame always. This flame is the eternal flame for the married couples.

Nonetheless, many times, one partner in the marriage holds back its progress. It is not appropriate; the second partner sits and sighs but continues to perform his part.

Before we marry, we make a vow to each other in the name of God and before our family and friends. Therefore, if someone is not performing his part and the marriage fails, there is going to be a curse upon him.

— Pius Yao Ashiara

Oh, let us pause a little and reflect on our life and organize our life and our homes to have good accountability of our life. Now let us listen, "Our homes as the Garden of Eden."

Our Homes as the Garden of Eden

Our homes are farms for our marriage. There we sow seeds that grow. Our homes are our Garden of Eden where we plant flowers and things that give us pleasure and happiness. There we take our marriage to live within.

When our marriage fails, our life and our nation fail. When we handle it well, it becomes a model for others to enter as well. Our homes are our Heaven on earth. That is why we must turn it into glory and jubilation. Dancing, laughter, love, respect, and applause make our homes a joy and pleasure.

We leave our homes in the mornings for work, leaving our homes empty. Sometimes problems confront us at work, by which we lose our joy and happiness before we return home. Problems at work should not create unhappiness for us that affect our joy at home. We must leave our problems at work by our door step before entering our homes.

— *Pius Yao Ashiara*

The Crown of Marriage

There is a crown we win in marriage. Whoever lives to the end of the marriage wins the crown. It is essential we live to the end of the marriage so that we can receive the crown, which we take to Heaven to account for the life we led in answer to God's assignment to us.

Marriage is God's order to us, which is to prove our performance on earth.

The Strong Pillars of Marriage

1. We must go into it with a good heart, pure mind, and clean hands.
2. We must take it with a good understanding.
3. We must take it by worshipping God in it.
4. We must build a strong fence with love around it, so that no wrong gets into it.
5. Its success must be our goal.
6. Frequent praying must be our concern all the time.
7. Our gratitude always to God while we are in it.

[These are a few words of wisdom to carry on our journey.]

[By this, we applaud all married couples. We wish them God's blessing in their journey. If we strictly

hold onto the advice and these words of wisdom, they will become our teacher, our father, our mother, our siblings, our friends, our advisers, our clergy, our psychiatrist, our hospital, our attorney, our judge, our Court of Justice, and a great school for us. Thanks to all.]

End

ABOUT THE AUTHOR

Pius Yao Ashiara studied business management at Rutgers University Newark, New Jersey. He has worked as a production executive in the publishing industry for the last twenty-eight years. Mr. Ashiara's 40-year study of people and their lives and marriages has brought about this work. He founded and operates the School for the Development of GREATMIND. He and his wife have been married for 34 years with three children.

Printed in the United States
By Bookmasters